JONNY ZUCKER has played in several bands and worked in radio, and as a stand-up comedian and a teacher. He started writing full-time and has now written over thirty books for adults, teenagers and children. These include the Venus Spring books for Piccadilly Press and the Max Flash series for Stripes. In addition to the Festival Time! series, he has also written *Dan and the Mudman* and *Striker Boy* for Frances Lincoln. He lives in London with his family.

JAN BARGER's previous titles include *Bible Stories for the Very Young*, and the Little Animals series.

For Fiona – J.Z.

First published in Great Britain in 2004 by
Frances Lincoln Limited, 4 Torriano Mews,
Torriano Avenue, London NW5 2RZ

www.franceslincoln.com

First paperback edition 2005

A catalogue record for this book is available from the British Library.

ISBN: 978-1-84507-294-0

Printed in China

9 8

The publishers would like to thank Rafiq Abdulla for acting as
consultant on this book and for writing the information page.

FESTIVAL TIME!

Sweet Dates to Eat

A Ramadan and Eid Story

Jonny Zucker

Illustrated by Jan Barger

FRANCES LINCOLN
CHILDREN'S BOOKS

It's the first day of Ramadan –
the ninth month in our Islamic year.
We remember how Mohammed
began to receive the words
of the Qur'an from Allah.

My older brother won't eat
or drink from dawn to sunset
for the whole month.
I am too young to fast.

Tonight I'm eating a delicious sweet date. It's the first thing our Prophet Mohammed ate after he fasted.

We hear the call to prayer
which tells us it's time
to go to the mosque.

It is the Night of Power when Allah
spoke the first words to Mohammed.
We pray and listen to the Qur'an
which is read aloud.

We look at the shining new moon
and know that Ramadan is over
and our festival of Eid can begin.

We enjoy a delicious feast
with our family and friends
to celebrate our festival of Eid.

What are Ramadan and Eid about?

As a Muslim, there are five things you must do. These are called the **Five Pillars of Islam**. They are:

- To declare that there is no God but Allah and that Mohammed is his prophet.
- To pray five times a day
- To give money to the needy. This is called **Zakat**.
- To fast during Ramadan.
- To make a pilgrimage (religious journey) to Mecca if possible.

Ramadan is a holy month. It was the month when the Prophet Mohammed received the first verses of the **Qur'an** (the Muslim holy text) from Allah. It is a time for reflection, for meditation, for carrying out additional prayers each evening, and for listening to the Qur'an being read in the mosque. The entire Qur'an is read by the time of the **Night of Power**. During Ramadan fasting begins at daybreak and ends at sunset. This means that you cannot eat or drink during this time. The Prophet Mohammed used to break his fast with a cup of water and a sweet date which restored some of the energy he lost during the day. He would pray before having a main evening meal.

Young children, people who are ill or on medication, and people who are travelling are not supposed to fast. Fasting is a sort of remembrance and it should not endanger your health.

Ramadan is a hard month and its end is met with the joy and pleasure of **Eid**. During Eid families visit each other, share a special meal and participate in a feeling of sharing with others and in a sense of achievement. It is a special time for children who are dressed up in new clothes and are given presents – there is a feeling of love and belonging. Eid is a celebration, a coming together, a return to nomal living after a period of personal reflection and spiritual renewal.